The Bad
Mothers

{"vey iz mir" is Yiddish for "woe is me"}

© 2017 Jana Zvibleman

Written and illustrated by Jana Zvibleman

All rights reserved. This book or any portion thereof may not be reproduced or used in any manner whatsoever without the express written permission of the publisher, except for the use of brief quotations in a book review.

Printed in the United States of America

ISBN: 978-1-944733-47-6

Back in the woods
the Bad Mothers gather,
growl, guffaw   the call
to congratulate themselves on their

Bad Bad jobs.

Monstrously thin or huge, lovely each
runs away to this nasty crowd   alone,

from all Directions,

gotten out of their children's hair at last.

They've come a long way, maybe
just to pat themselves on their backs,

with their terrible soft hands,

and celebrate

The Fear Mothers have made ready,

scrubbing and

spreading their fears around,

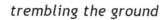

trembling the ground

Close behind them is heard, closer, closer,
the world-whimpering wail:
Whoa, the Worry Mothers.
"Oiy!" they chant, "Vey iz mere,
how I failed, you failed, they failed, we . . ."

The list is long. They toll
the bells:

    What Went

               Wrong

  and What Is

             Wrong

  and What Can Go

           Wrong

Tears 'til the Martyr Mother mourns
Who cares, I care, No One cares.

(Oh, how the Sighing Mothers sweetly sigh)

Now as the daughters and suns go down,
the rally cry "No one could have mothered worse!"

They laugh: they're done.

Their dances begin!

Some mothers tiptoe around everything,

some stomp on it all,

others push in where they don't belong,

Whooping an' Hollering.

For spoiling appetizers
the Bites·Their·Children's·Heads·Off Mothers clamp on
and sink their teeth in deep. They huddle to grumble
of chewing up children
but the bad taste is left in their mouths.

They spit it out,

and for just one more story time

gnash the Old Wives' tale of horror:

"Brats Bite Back"

A feast is brought on by the Smothering Mothers:
more casseroles they've baked offspring into.

They pour thick sauce over
recipes for disaster.

Lady Bad Mothers thank themselves graciously
They serve, serve, servings so rich, oh my Sweet Lard
set on the table right in your face.

The gravy spilleth over —

the children inside the dishes can't breathe.

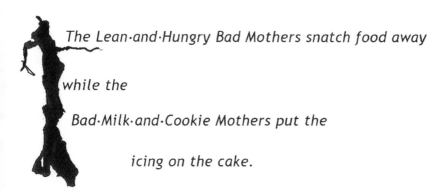

The Lean·and·Hungry Bad Mothers snatch food away

while the

Bad·Milk·and·Cookie Mothers put the

icing on the cake.

"Eat," they say, now to each other, Passing the Guilt

"Eat it anyway,

EAT,
darlings."

Yes, the Bad Mothers alone, together, recognize

the endless rituals

Come on, they shout, it's OUR turn! They start some games,
playing: Favorites

and Kick Back

and

Toss and Turn

and Hide YourSelf.

The scores: Lose/Lose

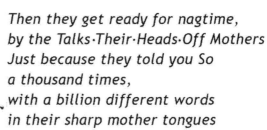

Then they get ready for nagtime,
by the Talks·Their·Heads·Off Mothers
Just because they told you So
a thousand times,
with a billion different words
in their sharp mother tongues
Be Careful, Be Good, and Can't, Don't and Do It Now

but

(no one is listening)

While the Mothers Who·Never·Said·

a·Word·About·It

stand off

and the Too·Busy Mothers busy themselves,

busy hands, busy bodies

and the big hippo·critical Mothers mutter
What Bad Mothers

Here, at dusk, even Long Gone Mothers and Absentee Mothers
dare to show their faces.   It's past time for make-up.
The Baby Sitters' fashion show shows them all
up. This is the Mothering Vogue,

Nanny Nanny Na Na

this is How To:
    they recite in horrible unison the experts' words:
Never pick up the little crier / Always pick up the little crier

Every Bad Mother ooos, coos, applauds:

the Bad Mothers Who Gave Up Everything,
the Bad Mothers Who Gave Up Nothing,
the Bad Mothers Who Gave Up
and Those Who Didn't, Did Not,

Never Will.

The Bad Mothers clap at the glossy display.
This season features
the freshest: Too·Young Mothers Who Knew No Better· and
the latest: Too·Old Mothers Who Just Can't Understand

The commentator never fails to mention that

whatever each did, in any color,

was Terribly, Fashionably

[Too tight / Too loose   Too long / Too short]

Unfit.

Stumped behind each tree, and under every rock-ing chair
are more Bad Mothers:

the Discount Mothers

and Just a Stage Mothers

and the Wire Monkey Surrogate Mothers

providing milk but

no fur

Bad Mothers, Bad Bad Mothers,

Now in the endless parade,

lugging on their backs the MotherLoad

Circling, waving homemade banners, manufactured threats,
things hidden behind curtains and faces.
Waves of remorse and waving grains of truth

tossing it all to the extreme Right

and
Leftovers Mothers.

Da-DA! (they hear the echo of the child's first word,
the child who always knew
Which parent was good) DA-DA!

The coronation of THE WORST MOTHER IN THE WORLD!

Every One of the Bad Mothers grabs her crown
accepting her scepter
Each lovingly dangerous Bad Mother Bear
protecting the idol,

raising high a
barefoot and pregnant

(don't tell her what she's in for)

Queen Bad Mother

It's Mother's Night:

       now they take back, unwrap, their own gifts

       and so finely:

        the Bad Mothers

          light the ceremonial fire

               under all

the old snapshots of their same old children,

          still pointing freud's fingers

     The Bad Mothers smell smoke,

      dancing around the blames,

celebrating,

HA

HA!

somewhere in the woods
we Bad Mothers go on

late, late into Ourselves at last.

Actually, Good Mothers

"All of these bad mothers are *me*."

"*I'm* certainly not a bad mother."

"Are you really saying the *kids* are bad?"

The Bad Mothers began as a lament. I felt sad and frustrated about ways that my children, at times over the years, decided that I had done them wrong. I also felt some guilt, that I had pointed the finger at my own mother, disdaining her as lacking.

And I thought about other daughters and sons, which means all of us. It's rare not to have learned all-too-well the misogyny of our culture. Can't balance your checkbook? Disappointed with your friends? Have a hangnail? The fault lies with your mother, of course. Good ol' Freud; yay the patriarchy.

Related are the "horizontal" judgements by some women. *That* mom on the playground is hovering. *That* one is neglectful. *She* is a "lawnmower" mother.

Which is not to say we don't ironically also revere mothers. The Madonna's modern personification, the pure, giving, perfection of womanhood: The Super Mother. Her very *raison d'être*, along with being the Good Wife, is to serve *us*, her offspring. She kisses our ow-ie, makes our appointments, spoons up our comfort food. We expect that she sacrifice her own desires, to accommodate ours. We actually demand it. We want our milk-and-cookies – and we want them now! Well, sooner or later, even such "good"

Moms are deemed failures: She made me dependent. She's such a martyr. What a toxic role model. In the 1970s, there was a saying: "The SuperMom image is dangerous, for all of us." Mothers who strived to anticipate and fulfill their children's every need, who juggled all domestic responsibilities and then some, plus made it in the male world, were "anti-feminist." They perpetuated the impossible myth that women must hold up everyone else; that we could do it all.

Ya just can't get it right. At least, not always.

So I pondered how we might grow beyond such stereotypes. Can women who have mothered ever come into their own? Can we slough off those scorns and blames, grow a new and thicker skin, and appreciate what we *have* done for the *benefit* of humanity? Can we get realistic, and forgive ourselves for our mistakes and weaknesses? Plus forgive our foremothers for theirs? Is there solace to be found in each other's tales?

Over the years, this Bad Mothers poem has indeed provided solace for many a woman. I've been thanked profusely for giving expression to a common, typically unspoken, angst. I've received tearful hugs. I've been told personal secrets. I've been asked to read the poem to gatherings of women.

And yet the Bad Mothers has also raised hackles. At a Red Hat luncheon of the generation of women who had been young mothers right after World War II, my reading elicited an uncomfortable silence. "I haven't the faintest what you mean," said one indignant listener. "*We* were such *good* mothers."

And at another reading, mothers of babies and toddlers looked at me blankly. Each was brilliantly creating her ideal of family. Damn, *they* were not bad mothers, and *never* would they be. Then, the room was abuzz with how they must counteract the shortcomings of *their* Moms . . ..

I don't mind the bristling or the non-identifying. Art can serve us by being controversial: let's look right at this difficult topic; bring on the discussions.

Many a mother between those extremes is uplifted by The Bad Mothers – especially those who have maneuvered through a child's stages of rudeness, at any age; *most* especially, those who have survived the parenting of teens. The caricatures resonate with mothers, who say, "I was busy working to make our living, and so they call me neglectful." "I was that casserole mother, and my children snickered about me." "My kid doesn't appreciate my saying even, 'Be careful.'"

They, those sons and daughters, don't *get* it.

If *you* do *get* it, I'm sorry that you are in our club. But hey, come on and laugh about it with us! We're in *good* company!

Made in United States
Troutdale, OR
10/07/2024

23501988R00015